THE

BLACKSPEECH

THE
BLACKSPEECH

KEBONYEMODISA MBONI REYNOLDS MOTHUPI

BY THE SAME AUTHOR

MOJANALA – THE TOURIST; Ja nala le rona

FOREWORD

Kebonyemodisa Reynolds Mothupi is a poet of note whose voice we can only ignore at our own great peril. His is the voice of a young and emerging poet who, as none other than the great African writer and poet Chinua Achebe taught us, is on a mission to fulfill his role as both teacher and healer in the community. He does this by shining his light on us in order to give us direction and hope when only gloom, despair and utter darkness seem to be the only options on the table.

Hence in this collection of poems – an oeuvre and body of work ranging in focus from themes of romantic love, male contrition at lost love, condemnation of poverty and social injustice, a rejection of racism and an affirmation of our common humanity to a celebration of the life and work of author Bessie Head whom he describes as a 'woman ahead of her time' and whose words and writings will continue to resonate future generations even after she herself has long departed this world.

The reader will find that there is something for everyone, lessons to be gleaned from the poet as teacher and conscience of his society, by all and sundry, from different walks of life.

This is certainly a book worth reading, for it provides us with the right coordinates as we navigate our increasingly complex world of economic modernization and cultural globalization.

-   *Kagiso Senthufhe*

INTRODUCTION

The Black speech is a collection of poems based on the reality of life.

They have varying themes that range from but are not limited to relationships, racism, love, unity, education, poverty, motivation, praise and worship.

It is my sincerest hope that the reader will be immersed in the depth of each poem.

- Kebonyemodisa Mboni Reynolds Mothupi

TABLE OF CONTENTS

THE BLACK SPEECH

Exploration that bred exploitation,
Bread of life snatched from our hands
Cunning and sugar coated administration,
Maladministration they spat on our lands
In the name of colonization resources depleted,
Cultures evaded, sculptures left behind,
The mission fully completed.

Blackshipped into slavery,
A black sheep White considered Black,
Days were dark, Black had no calvary,
Cruel is the rife sea side lining Black,
No more perennial rivers of welfare,
Motherland Africa, the best habitat,
All the reality is bitter warfare,
No more rest for your inhabitants,

Reynolds Mothupi

Invented   blood   battle   disunites
brotherhood

Undeveloped continent you remain yet rich
Heavily pregnant you are with minerals,
Discarded down the drain, themselves they
enrich,
All we experience is perennial funerals,
The mother of skills and Innovation,
Wasted all in vain and pain
Intentionally washed from the heads,
Africa,the pioneer of civilization
Confusion and competition bitterly instilled
in hearts,

To the little white cat,
Belittle not the black cat,
The covered will be uncovered;
It is not over 'till it is over
Unity we shall recover and empower,
Indistinguishable supremacy is on the verge
Vicious and Sharp edged

like a knife edge
We shall not revenge,
But unity convey to obey.

To the little black cat,
Hurt not humanity,
Peace act,
Chase not after wind,
Mind other faces though different races,
Bitter reality,
Actions leave traces,
Reject racism embrace and race human race.

Sons and daughters of the soil,
We shall not rot we are not alone,
In one accord we shall overcome the tall toil,
Black is a colour, white is a colour,
Red is our blood, same are we as one,
It shall rain peace
Aswe reign supreme in unity parlour,

A   big   no   to   racism,   we   are   one

A   big   no   to   racism,   we   are   one

MY BELOVED PRESIDENT

A natural born leader he is ceaselessly at his prime
Tough like a rock he stood the test of time
Wholly endowed with great leadership skills,
High skills running through his thick red blood,
Laziness and unproductivity he kills,
My president the one and only he controls the flood,

A true son of the soil, he stands out tall,
A mustard seed that sprung from the revered Chieftainship lineage,
He will never ever fall,

The great lineage of Chiefs starting with The
great Khama himself,
SeretseKhamaIanKhama, the 1st born son
of the great Sir SeretseKhama,
For his nation he sacrifices self,
An adventurous and ever present president

He listens and advices correctly
None is like Khama He is Karma to his
political adversaries,
Diverse people he unites coherently
A dignified gentleman, he believes in dignity
for progression,
Never is he short sighted of discipline,
In his leadership exists no regression,
Unity definesthe Botswana he so deeply
loves deeply

Democracy his priority,
People first, foreign to him is minority,
He rules with quality and equality,
Development he drives with passion

A father of the nation with deep compassion
His leadership drives and thrives the economy,
My president, Yes he is my president

Non-tolerant to alcohol and drugs,
Humanity he loves and hugs
A lover of people,
Very generous at heart,
Hate is not his taste,
Hate him or love him,
Forever he will be engraved in our hearts.
Yes,He is my beloved President
He is Lieutenant General Dr Seretse Khama Ian Khama

CRY NOT SWEETHEART

Gallons of tears going down your cheeks,
Blood filled vessels tense and ready to
burst,
All because of my fault and side kicks,
Deep down in my heart you are the best
Lovel never meant to hurt you,
I hate me for the hurt now,

From your heart I will never default nor
revolt
In my floral chest, rest on a crest
You and I will never defect,
An unbreakable pact,matter of fact
With true love I will satisfy thine heart,
Forever you will be my part

Reynolds Mothupi

It's crystal clear my dear,
You are my super star,
Destined to be the queen of my empire,
Our love snow white without tar,
You are my fire and desire
My legion will testify,
You are my religion,
Cry not sweetheart,
You are my heart

REALISTIC POVERTY

All day long the poor lament silently,
Their life is spent in hardship and sorrow,
On deaf ears their cry fall relentlessly,
Bitter is the penetration to the bone marrow,
Poverty is written all over their bodies,
They work for food when there is no food for work,
In the midst of strife they strive to survive

Lamentations of the poor-a far cry to the state
Pathetic is their deterioration of health,
Pain and vain they taste,
Horrible is their state,

Never in life have the poor tasted wealth,
The poor and rich play not together
Lavish lives ofleaders overlooking the poor,
only remembered for elections
Poorpoor their votes they pour, only to be
denied connections and selections
Words are sweet but never replace poverty

Poverty is not and never will it be our
culture
Down with poverty down,
Let we impregnate the soil
Together let we implement in substantial
agriculture
Down with poverty down,
For a great course let we toil
Fold not your arms and slumber,
Weed poverty and breed beasts
Stand on your own,
Firmly as a family member
Gird yourself with hard work armor,
Work begets great feasts.

Disagree with the toilet,
Fend for yourself,
Get lazy and poverty becomes your master
Let self-reliance define your shelf
Poverty is not yours be a superstar
Work hard, accumulate property,
Let's unite and eradicate poverty

TAKE NO LIFE, LIFE GOES ON

Sole dream of my life was she to my part
Wholeheartedly I adored her breed
The beautiful lady, the queen of my heart
In my heart existed no greed
Adornments and gifts showered I upon her front
Her dark secrets I could not read
It is over she uttered in the front yard

My vessels boiled the blood pressure
The conclusion to pull the trigger
My heart thus emptied of pleasure
Charged I 'to help with a gold digger',
No stop!!!!No stop!!! It is not right,
Tools down spare lives dear,
Brave is a man with a bright light clear,

Reynolds Mothupi

Hush, take no life as life goes on,
Appreciated, valued you are to the society's
join,
Best to jawjawthan be war war drawn
Killings bring no solution but pain
Save your life and her ladyship own,
Peace, love and joy proclaim

Life goes on, let live and let go
Bright and incredible is your future
Take no life for life goes on
Hold on to life, have a great life adventure,
Love and unity is your nature,

You are the man, let live and let go
Not to 'passion killings' No
True love we must nurture and treasure
Thou shall not kill, let live and let go

THE LORD MY GOD

The Lord my God Almighty, king of kings
Your love evenly spread throughout the
world
I find comfort and refuge under your wings
Spiritually nourished I am through your
word
The Lord my God you are the greatest

There is none like you, you are mighty
You rule the world with order
My Lord the eternal light that shines
brightly
In your creation there is no disorder
The Lord my God you are the greatest

Like a baby I sleep in your loving arms
What a caring God, He truly understands
Firmly the earth rests upon your palms

Reynolds Mothupi

Whenever I am down, by my side my God
stands
The Lord my God you are the greatest

Thank you Lord for being my God
Without you there is no life
You treasure humanity more than gold
Your presence vanishes strife
The Lord my God you are the greatest

BESSIE HEAD-THE HEAD OF THE NATION

A TRIBUTE TO BESSIE HEAD

From the east to the west your words
stretch across,
Marvelous and beautiful like a red rose,
From north to south they flow like sweet
honey
Great writings that cannot be bought with
money
The rock that stood the test of the time
Bessie Head, the head of the nation

A great phenomenal woman of substance,
Nothing compares to your artistic literature
Indeed you are an excellent teacher
Always busy writing, you were a busy bee

Reynolds Mothupi

In our minds you created places we would
love to be
Bessie Head, the head of the nation

Blessed are we to have you as a head
Our dry land you quenched with heavy rains
of words,
Desirable words that construct the soul,
Strong words that unite the nation,
Together as one we will remain, never to
break apart
Bessie Head, the head of the nation

Prime time you dedicated to literature
Nations marvel at your majestic works
Birds astonished,
Melodiously sing to your words
A woman ahead of her time
Your writings are a gold mine
You are a true head,
a head that leads the nation

Behind you left legacy,
Legacy of greatness
You might be gone but your writings live on
Bessie Head the head of the nation

PULA!!!!!!PULA!!!!!!!PULA!!!!!!!!!!
TRI BUTE TO OUR GREAT WRITER
MAY YOUR SOUL REST IN PEACE

Reynolds Mothupi

SUFFER NOT THE CHILDREN

Healthy and lovely, with a bright smile they come around,
Sadly with pathetic faces they enter the ground,
Somebody tell me, how could it be?
Young and innocent they giggle awaiting hardship,
Daily torment from ferocious wolves,
Suffer not the beautiful children

Children, a precious gift, why suffer them, why?
Worn out and sad, like the Sahara they look dry,
To that gorgeous child plant tender love,

Let the child shine like a snow white dove,
They live to endure child slavery not to enjoy life,
Chained and engaged in hard labour,
Suffer not the beautiful children

Child abuse, the order of the day,
The world is starved of loving adults
Together let we eradicate child abuse.
Irresponsible adults molest children,
The world is sick, why suffer the little angels?
Innocently born with the virus they are born to suffer,
Suffer not the little children, responsible let we be

What have they done? Why suffer children?
Open that heart of yours and reach out,
Reach out to love suffering children,
Let us give them the love they deserve

Children are the future that we must preserve,
Suffer not the little children,
Every adult must be a parent to children,
United nations reach out and help,

Help fight child abuse bitterly,
Eliminate child slavery, demolish child molestation,
True love and care reflected in demonstration
Let we fight and eliminate child soldiers hypocrisy,
Carry the children on our shoulders, they need democracy not hypocrisy,
Suffer not the precious children

THE MINE UNDER

In your mind, undermine nobody,
We all possess great, great potential,
Mind your neighbours, undermine nobody,
Recognition of all, quite essential

Deep down the mine riches we mine,
Represent one another entirely
Experts be individuals their way,
Respect fellow man heartily
The same flesh are we,
Men not undermine

No man is dead wood in the neighborhood,
Deep down the mine diamonds we find,
Let peace reign and uplift brotherhood,
Wealthy is every man's mind,
Equality rules, undermine a man not

Reynolds Mothupi

Black or white, men not undermine
Rich or poor are we the same,
Deep down the skin are we as one,
Humanity is all but our name,
Men not undermine
Magnificent and rich is every mind!

United in diversity in human university,
Externally different,internally indifferent
You neither black nor white but human,
Say bye to bygones let them be bygones,
Venture into united culture future,
Men not under mine,
Deep down the mineriches we mine.

PUT THAT WOMAN FIRST

She is your first not your last make her the
best among the rest,
The queen of your heart she is, let her reign
supreme,
Put that woman first, if you truly love her,
Love her like you loved none before
Like a glass handle her with care,
Look into her almond eyes and your love
declare
Call her a pet name as you pat her back
Let no one take her place for she is your
only, give her true love,
Man, put that woman first she is the best,
Nothing beats her,
If you put her first there will be neither
cheating nor hating

Respect, love and care convey to that woman, she is all yours
When tears fall from her eyes, wipe them with your heart,
Show her real love; stand by her side in good times and bad times
 Don't be deceived, one bird in your hand is worth more than two in the forest

Put that woman first,
Smile at her and give her tender kisses
Whisper sweet nothings into her ears
Let her hear your heart beat oozing with love,
Put that woman first,
She is your treasure give her all the pleasure,
Play with her, have fun and make her laugh as you give her royal treatment,
Remain loyal to that woman, she is all yours

SONG OF HAPPINESS

Gone is the sorrow I had a while ago
A bright future I will hold and unfold me to
happiness as I sing a song of happiness
It was sad a while ago now joy fills my heart
thus I am emptied of sadness
I will embrace and race the song of
happiness

To the dark past with its sorrows goodbye
To the bright future with its happiness,
Here I come,
I will wear a smile and nothing will take
away my joy as I enjoy
Enjoying the fun with endurance and
making hay while the sun shines

Reynolds Mothupi

Passion and purpose I discovered,
No more fear, with joy I am powered,
Purposely focused on the vertical dimension
of life,
Happiness is my trusted and beloved wife.

REFUGEE TEARS

Vividly I remember the dark and bloody day,
Alone, naïve and fragile left for dead,
Poverty, pain and starvation are the order of the day,
Uncontrollable tears rolling down my cheeks,
A loner I stand, no one to wipe the gushing tears as grief tears my soul,
Civil war wiped all but me,
The entire family swallowed by death on earth.

A lone ranger in the camp,
In my heart sorrow camped
Bitter days rain down on my empty soul
My empty stomach roars and cracks like thunder,

Reynolds Mothupi

Under my scrawny body there is no peace,
I long for better days,
Peace keepers try to bring peace,
My great loss they cannot replace
No man can contain my struggle,
My tough life I had behind a laugh

Irreplaceable is my thick blood,
My family, my refuge,
So priceless that the refugee camp cannot
replace,
I might be alive but I am dead,
On earth I have no place,
My bloodless heart is filled with dread,
My miseries have no end ohhh, why me?
Why me God?
How long shall I suffer?Why am I odd?

GO TO SCHOOL

The essential education fountain
The life light that brightly shines
Higher than the ground climb the life
mountain
School the key to good living,
By crawling a child learns to stand,
The essence and presence of education
understand

No matter how hard keep moving,
He who learns will keep on improving,
When you break down,
Fight on like a soldier
Complete your courses completely,
Do it all the way,
Taste education life,
Lean on her shoulder

Reynolds Mothupi

To gel lost is to learn the way

By trying often the monkey learns to jump
across the trees,
Through school you pay all the due fees,
Read and plant seeds,
Great rewards you shall reap,
Praise upon you nations shall heap,
Don't be empty inside like an empty drum

Wake up and go to school, wake up
Enlighten your mind through education
Get up and go to school-get up
Leave no room for miseducation
Have room for miss education
Let her be your queen
Leave room for Mr Education
Let him be your king

School is not a fallacy
Education is a matter of urgency
Now I know education is legacy
Study hard with diligence,
Taste the beauty of school,
Learning expands great souls
School-The light that guides through the dark

LIFE ACCORDING TO ME

Life is a mystery,
It is not how long you live,
Life is not determined by history
It is not based on how you live,
Life is life I say, it is what it is.
Believe it, it is life.
The same rain that flourishes flora catalysis
catastrophe

An individual's life determines not their
destiny,
A brutal death you can die while a perfect
life you lead,
Lead a shameful life, a peaceful death you
may encounter,
Riches you may have yet walking dead,

Poverty you may wear but living large at heart,
What is life that man can't express?
Life is lifeI say,
The same sun that melts wax hardens clay

Life is a mixture of love and hate
It is a concoction of bliss and pain,
It is a stormy rain that pours without a pause,
An endless joy to be enjoyed, incessant hardship to be endured,
A salty and sweet stream it is,
Goodness gracious, how can it be?

Whatever you think about Life, it's your ideology
To me life is a mystery beyond feeble minds, it is not astrology
A deep rooted mystery planted in the heavens above

Life is life thunderously
I say and clearly declare
No formula unlocks the life puzzle,
I marvel at the amazing life maze

TO MY DARLING

You are not a mistaken identity
Your first glance converted me to a believer
You planted in me a seed of reality
Reality that showed me the meaning of true
love
White and pure as a snow white dove

You made me believe that two different
hearts could merge
You are indeed a perfect match
You and I met and the best of both worlds
emerged
Can't imagine a match without you

Whenever you are down, I will uplift you
 Stretch out your hand let me hold you
Let us gracefully march towards love land
In great abundance we shall land.

Reynolds Mothupi

FLYING WITHOUT WINGS

A tough journey encountered I,
All my ways lead to darkness,
In all my breakthroughs a leak emerged,
My future seemed very bleak and black
In my soul misfortune camped,
I laid hopelessly with a crashed heart

One day my heart unlocked
Versatility I discovered deep down within
On the plateau I stood on my two's as I took
off
Flying without wings
My dark past I left behind,
An everlasting bright future I embraced

A sad night covers me no more,
A highflying knight I am,
Flying gracefully without wings

To a wide blue sky turned my dark clouds,
The rocky and steeply journey is no more
Never will I land on that sorrowful land,
Without wings I will fly higher and higher,

Misfortune tarries a night
But joy comes in the morning
Unleash the massive strength within your heart,
The greatest strength of a role model
On top I will stay never to go downnever.

The magnificent strength
Of flying without wings
Flying without wings to achieve the unachievable
Flying without wings to break records
Flying without wings going for the stars
Flying without wings
O' yes I'm flying without wings

Believe in yourself
You are the greatest
Anything is possible and achievable.....
Impossible is possible

THE ŒND